My Mindful A to Zen

Krina Patel-Sage

For Oscar and Roman

Lantana

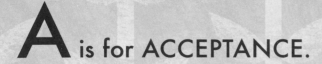

A is for ACCEPTANCE.

When things make us sad
and plans go wrong, that's OK.
Better days will come.

B is for BEING.

Just being yourself,
doing nothing, is enough.
Be content with you.

C is for CREATIVITY.

Making things is fun!
Getting busy with your hands
brings joy to the heart.

D is for DANCING.

When the music plays,
feel the rhythm and move your
body to the beat!

F is for FRIENDSHIP.

Playing with our friends:
everyone is welcome here.
We were all new once.

G is for GRATITUDE.
What makes you happy?
Think of the things you love and
be thankful for them.

H is for HUGS.

Wrap your arms around
in a warm, cosy embrace.
Hugging shows your love.

I is for IMAGINATION.
Let your mind drift to places afar. Where will your thoughts take you today?

J is for JOINING IN.
Working together,
side by side, makes us stronger.
We shape tomorrow.

K is for KARMA.
Your hard work pays off.
The energy you put in
grows into rewards.

L is for LETTING GO.

Bad feelings happen;
accept them and release them.
Let happiness shine.

M is for MISTAKES.

Sometimes things go wrong;
gather strength and keep learning.
It's OK to fail.

N is for NATURE.

Respect and value creatures and their habitats. Notice small wonders.

O is for OM.

Lift your spirit with
the sound of the Universe:
sacred vibration.

Q is for QUESTIONS.

Curiosity
builds the mind. If you don't know,
ask someone who does.

R is for READING.

Books hold the power
to take us to a new world.
Enjoy the journey.

S is for SMILING.
Beaming smiles spread light from one face to another, making connections.

T is for TIDYING.

You've had fun and made a mess! Now it's time to put things back for next time.

U is for UPCYCLING.

Bringing new beauty
to something old saves pennies
and saves our planet.

V is for VOLUNTEERING.

Giving up your time
for those in need of a friend
shows them that you care.

W is for WAITING.

Things can take longer
than we would like. When we wait,
patience rewards us.

X is a KISS.

Sleepy goodnight kiss,
cheerful peck hello, or just
because I love you.

Y is for YOGA.

Quietly focus,
stretch and breathe. Yoga takes care
of body and mind.

Z is for ZEN.

Gently close your eyes;
let the world drift around you.
It's time to relax.

Each entry in this book highlights one or more of the "Five Ways to Wellbeing," shown below. These are steps that have been proven to boost mental health, increase positivity, and help us get the best out of life.

Connect **Be Active** **Take Notice** **Keep Learning** **Give**

First published in the United Kingdom in 2021 by Lantana Publishing Ltd.
www.lantanapublishing.com | info@lantanapublishing.com

American edition published in 2021 by Lantana Publishing Ltd., UK.

Text & Illustration © Krina Patel-Sage, 2021

The moral rights of the author-illustrator have been asserted.

Distributed in the United States and Canada by Lerner Publishing Group, Inc.
241 First Avenue North, Minneapolis, MN 55401 U.S.A.
For reading levels and more information, look for this title at www.lernerbooks.com
Cataloging-in-Publication Data Available.

Hardback ISBN: 978-1-911373-80-3
eBook PDF: 978-1-911373-84-1
ePub3: 978-1-913747-52-7

Printed and bound in China
Original artwork created using mixed media, completed digitally